A Teaspoon of Courage

Other Books by Bradley Trevor Greive

The Blue Day Book

The Blue Day Journal and Directory

Dear Mom

Looking for Mr. Right

The Meaning of Life

The Incredible Truth About Mothers

Tomorrow

Priceless: The Vanishing Beauty of a Fragile Planet

The Book for People Who Do Too Much

Friends to the End

Dear Dad

The Simple Truth About Love

Children's Books

The Blue Day Book for Kids

Friends to the End for Kids

A Teaspoon
of Courage

A Little Book of Encouragement
for Whenever You Need It

BRADLEY TREVOR GREIVE

**Andrews McMeel
Publishing, LLC**

Kansas City

07 08 09 10 TWP 10 9 8 7 6 5 4

ISBN-13: 978-0-7407-5472-2
ISBN-10: 0-7407-5472-6

Library of Congress Control Number: 2006923125

Attention: Schools and Businesses
Andrews McMeel books are available at quantity discounts with bulk purchase for educational, business, or sales promotional use. For information, please write to: Special Sales Department, Andrews McMeel Publishing, LLC, 4520 Main Street, Kansas City, Missouri 64111.

Photo Credits
Acclaim Images (USA)—www.acclaimimages.com
Anders Geidemark (Sweden)—anders.geidemark@telia.com
Auscape International (Australia)—www.auscape.com.au
Australian Picture Library (Australia)—www.australianpicturelibrary.com.au
Austral International (Australia)—www.australphoto.com.au
BIG Australia (Australia)—www.bigaustralia.com.au
BTG Studios (Australia)—www.btgstudios.com
Chandoha Photography (UK)—www.chandohaphotography.com
Frans Lanting Photography (USA)—www.lanting.com
Gerald Hinde—hinde@netactive.co.za
Getty Images (Australia)—www.gettyimages.com
Norvia Behling (USA)—www.foxhillphoto.com
Pavel German Wildlife Images (Australia)—www.australiannature.com
Photolibrary.com (Australia)—www.photolibrary.com
Ron Kimball Studios (USA)—www.ronkimballstock.com
Stock Photos (Australia)—www.stockphotos.com.au
Wildlight Photo Agency (Australia)—www.wildlight.net

Detailed page credits for the remarkable photographers whose work appears in *A Teaspoon of Courage* and other books by Bradley Trevor Greive are freely available at www.btgstudios.com.

For Thomas N. Thornton.

A man whose boundless creativity and courage
has nurtured a galaxy of creative stars,
brought disparate nations together as one family,
built a wine cellar that humbles and enthralls,
and won the heart of a woman who
wrestles bagpipes and makes moonshine.

TNT, you are an inspiration to us all.

ACKNOWLEDGMENTS

Readers who know me might assume that since I have roughly the same amount of scar tissue and artificial joints as the greatest Spanish bullfighter, Manuel "El Cordobés" Benítez, I might actually know or thing or two about courage. This is not so. I am, however, a self-taught expert on postoperative rehabilitation, and I have a few pieces of worthwhile advice for anyone who might want to take up skydiving or desert racing or get extremely close to aggressive wild animals, as I once did.

The point is that while obstacles, danger, heartache, injustice, and rampant stupidity abound in the modern world, genuine courage seems to be in short supply. When I considered this unpleasant disparity, it seemed clear that from time to time, we could all use a shot of unfiltered courage to get past the challenges life regularly throws down at our feet—I know I could—and that, quite simply, is how this little book began.

I have the good fortune of working with the most inspiring individuals every single day. All of them, through word and deed, made this book very easy to write. At the top of this stellar list I must make special mention of three personal heroes—Chris Schillig, Jane Palfreyman, and Anita Arnold.

I also want to thank all the photographers and their agents who contributed the images that bring my modest text to life. I encourage everyone interested in their world-class photography to seek out the updated contact details posted at www.btgstudios.com.

Of course *courage*, in every abstract and tangible sense, is utterly embodied in the character of my literary agent and life coach, Sir Albert J. Zuckerman of Writers House, New York. Al grew up during America's great depression and showed, even at the tender age of eight, that he was made of stern stuff. To support his family, little Al worked three, sometimes four, six-hour shifts each day sweeping floors at his father's hat factory, running errands for small business owners, and (under a pseudonym and false mustache) advising the city government how best to develop its infrastructure policy. Al's unyielding stance on the social benefit of centralized, publicly owned mass transport systems earned him the name "Old Iron Whiskers."

One evening while walking home from a spirited bull session with Governor Franklin D. Roosevelt, young Albert was accosted by three hired goons sent to influence him in favor of an opportunistic consortium's plan to privatize the fledgling subway system. Al held his ground despite being outweighed in the contest by more than two hundred pounds per man. The biggest thug caught him with a sucker punch that sent him reeling and almost dislodged his famous whiskers. But the mustache stayed true and so did Al. He counterattacked like a furious gamecock, dashing between the splayed legs of his taller, heavier opponents and lashing out at their shins and knees with the thick, keen-edged soles of his platform boots even as he maintained a flurry of sharp uppercuts.

When Al shares this story with me, he always emphasizes the maxim "Fortune favors the brave." At that exact moment when his fate hung in the balance, a mangy clutch of alley cats, panicked by the commotion, leaped from their Dumpster. By pure chance, they landed smack on the bare heads of the three goons who, under a violently hissing crown of sharp claws and fishy fangs, gave up their malevolent mission and ran howling down the alley.

It's no surprise that since that day, Al never has been without his trademark false mustache and has always shared his New York home with the biggest cat he can find. The last time I dined at his table, we finished our meal with coffee and vintage port as Sir Albert sat contentedly beside the fire stroking Rufus, a gigantic ginger feline that resembles a dwarf tiger more than any domestic pet.

"You see, my boy," Al said quietly, "Courage is not always something to be sought on the meanest of streets or in the darkest of nights. It is actually something that we celebrate and draw comfort from within our hearts and homes. I don't have to confront peril to know courage—no one does. I simply pat Rufus, and I feel secure and content that whatever happens, I will do what is right. For me, the mustache has become a symbol of indubitable purpose and indomitable spirit. I know that I can and will rise to face any challenge in the best possible way. I ask no more of myself or any man, woman, or child, and I am happy in the knowledge that my dreams shall prevail if it is right that they should do so."

Sir Albert, your false mustache is a symbol of strength for the whole world. Long may your "Iron Whiskers" of courage gleam brightly.

A Teaspoon of Courage

Sooner or later everyone runs up against a brick wall.

You could hit trouble at home or at work and get wiped out emotionally and physically. Suddenly, it seems possible that all your efforts might be for nothing. It's not a good feeling,

and only Hollywood's best cosmetic surgeon
could put a smile back on your face.

Your aching, disillusioned head seems completely empty of ideas.

The anxiety builds up, and your brain
feels like it will explode out of your eyes and ears.

Everything grinds to a halt.

It's hard to believe this could happen to you.
You started out so alert and eager, poised for success.

But somehow, no matter how hard you try,
the things you desire most are always just out of reach.

To make things worse, it seems as if life is getting more difficult.
The bar keeps getting raised for no good reason.

It feels like no one wants you to succeed—
as if the whole world is staring down its nose at you.

For many people, it's all a bit too much, and they try to drown their sorrows in cheap wine or fine champagne.

They give up on their dreams and themselves.
Tiny sobs will echo in their empty hearts for the rest of their lives.

Other people simply refuse to acknowledge that a problem exists.
They figure if they can't see it, maybe it will just vanish,
like a scary ghost.

But you can't take a sick day from destiny.

So instead of shriveling up inside your fear and disappointment
and disappearing from the civilized world,

it's much better to come out and face the music.

Of course, putting on a brave face is only half the battle.

There is nothing wrong with a little cheeky optimism,

but confidence, which is merely the appearance of courage,
is often just a mask.

Like splashing on liberal quantities of cheap cologne,
confidence can only conceal some of the truth.

Looking brave is a lot easier than being brave. Even cowards can just furrow their brows, grit their teeth, and thrust out their jaws. 23

They can adopt a wrestler's stance and lay down a challenge
to the whole world. People like this often intimidate others
to appear fearless and powerful.

"Watch it, pig. I'm walkin' here!"

Of course, true courage doesn't mean losing your sensitivity.

Whether you know it or not, you were born tough enough
to tackle anything important in life.

You should take comfort from the fact that you have
enormous potential in reserve if you ever need it.

Courage does not mean being without fear.
Courage means acting in spite of fear. Fear is healthy.

Those who seem utterly fearless usually don't know what's going on. In fact, confidence levels are often directly proportional to ignorance.

The world is a scary place sometimes, and it is smart
to be cautious and evaluate the risks before you act on a plan.
Hey, Rome wasn't built in a day, and the lunar landings
weren't organized over a holiday weekend.

Courage is something you develop over a lifetime.
Sure, some young people are singled out as future leaders
because of their outgoing personalities or the way they look,
but when they finally face up to real life . . .

"Aiiieeee, a baby mouse!"

On the other hand, many folks are written off as crybabies
or basket cases because they aren't tall enough or smart enough
or funny enough or athletic enough or whatever.

But when the world turns inside out, they may well be among the few who can stare down the challenge without blinking.

Doing things that are inherently dangerous
does not necessarily indicate courage.
For example, swimming with sharks is, if not an extremely
unfortunate coincidence, just plain stupid.

Roller Derby is similarly indicative of poor judgment,

as is starting your own religion in order
to claim generous tax benefits.

An example of genuine bravery would be the heroic soldier
who volunteers for a dangerous mission to spare his friends.

Other examples of courage might be less bold, but are no less worthy. A brave person is someone who speaks the truth even when she knows it won't be popular.

A brave person is someone who believes in himself
and is ready to go it alone if he must.

A brave person is prepared not to get a nose job.

A brave person is able to say, "Good lord, my butt looks big in these pants. I'm gonna join a gym!"

A brave person would swallow her pride
and apologize after a painful misunderstanding

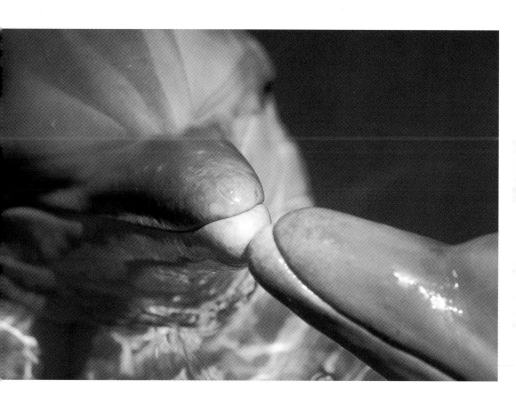

or hold his fears in check long enough to steal that first tender kiss.

Truly brave individuals slowly but surely rebuild their lives after suffering profound personal losses.

The most important example of real courage is having the strength
to pursue our dreams in a world full of obstacles and excuses.

Of course, many people think this means the ability to hang in there when things get tough, and in some life situations, it's true that just surviving is a major victory.

However, in life there is only "forward" and "backward."
It's one or the other. After you've regained your breath,
licked your wounds, and reevaluated the situation,
"hanging in there" just means you are not going forward.

And if you are going nowhere, you're as close to failing
as you are to succeeding. What can you possibly achieve
from this precarious position?

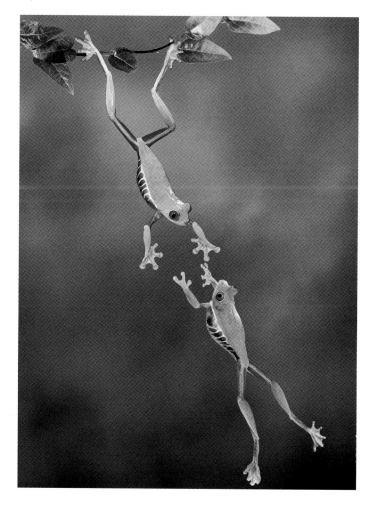

Do you plan to just hang around
until someone truly brave comes to your rescue?

Or until hostile onlookers gather and start to shout,
"Jump! Jump! Jump!"?

It is said that all good things come to those who wait,
and patience is a virtue, but nothing good ever comes to those
who sit on their ever-increasing butts.

Dreams don't stand still,
and if your dreams are swimming upstream,

then that's where you should probably be heading.
Whether it's the pursuit of health, wealth, or the love of your life,
"pursuit" is the key word.

55

Everyone has days when they feel they have reached their limits.

Sometimes the obstacles just seem to be too much.

Heroes cry, too.

But they don't quit on themselves. Ever.

Consider the grim fact that all over the world, people are sleeping on streets and inside bus shelters. They have a million more reasons to believe they've run out of options than you do.

Now look yourself in the eye and ask yourself if you've tried everything. Have you really given it all your creative energy?

If you honestly have, then you are entitled to curl into a minute,
sniveling ball and take up as little space in the world
as is humanly possible.

Or you might remind yourself who you are by saying, "I am not perfect, but I am someone who learns from my mistakes."

"I am willing to sacrifice for that which really matters.
I am true to my word, and I am proud to be me."

"I admit that I am curiously attractive,
but I am not just a pretty face."

"I will achieve what I say I will achieve. I will find a way forward no matter what setbacks occur."

"Because I am not a quitter."

"I AM NOT A QUITTER!"

Every time you reaffirm your faith in yourself, it grows stronger,

while simultaneously, anything that kept you down and
held you back grows weaker and weaker and weaker.

Stand tall and march proudly toward your goals and dreams
with your shoulders squared and your head held high.

Barriers that seemed insurmountable

will become surmountable, maybe even a cakewalk.

This may not happen in the wink of an eye.
In fact, it might take days, weeks, months—who knows?

The landscape of our lives is vast and varied.

But as long as you are moving forward, if only by inches,
it doesn't matter what lies in front of you.
You will get where you are going in the end.

A journey of a thousand miles and a Latin dance marathon both begin with a single step.

The world's greatest symphony starts with one solitary note.

Of course, even while composing the world's greatest symphony,
you can still feel like you are pushing poop uphill.

And even if you are moving forward on your life journey, you might sometimes feel like you want to stop the world and get off.

You *will* make mistakes and you *will* look stupid—we all do.
That is part of the process.

Mean people with bad teeth and narrow-set eyes
will laugh at your blunders. That's part of it, too.

Don't let anger, frustration, and embarrassment ruin your plans.

If you have to, stick your head in ice water to defog your brain.

Visualize your goal and imagine how good you will feel
if you actually achieve it.

Don't waste precious time and energy looking backward or worrying about naysayers. You'll just trip yourself up.

Do take advantage of spare moments to reevaluate your strategy.
You might have to alter your flight path to avoid heavy weather.

Then dig deep and set out again and again and again
until you make it.

And you will make it. If you just keep paddling,
your wave will arrive to take you all the way in to the beach.

You will find your holy grail.

When that happens, you will be deafened by the cheering of
celestial hosts

and surrounded by an adoring public.

Or you can sit quietly by yourself
and savor the moment with a nice cup of tea.

Best of all, you can experience the peaceful satisfaction that
comes when you are true to yourself. For you will be one of those
rare individuals who truly live their dreams.

You will be someone who has the courage to seek out anything
that stirs your heart and soul. And when opposing forces
great and small shout out their dark challenge,
you will be able to answer calmly and clearly,

"Bring it on, baby!"